FUNNY JOKES FOR 9 YEAR OLD KIDS

100+ Crazy Jokes That Will Make You Laugh Out Loud!

Cooper the Pooper

© **Copyright 2021 Cooper the Pooper - All rights reserved.**

The content contained within this book may not be reproduced, duplicated or transmitted without direct written permission from the author or the publisher.

Under no circumstances will any blame or legal responsibility be held against the publisher, or author, for any damages, reparation or monetary loss due to the information contained within this book, either directly or indirectly.

Legal Notice:
This book is copyright protected. It is only for personal use. You cannot amend, distribute, sell, use, quote or paraphrase any part, or the content within this book, without the consent of the author or publisher.

Disclaimer Notice:
Please note the information contained within this document is for educational and entertainment purposes only. All effort has been executed to present accurate, up to date, reliable, complete information. No warranties of any kind are declared or implied. Readers acknowledge that the author is not engaged in the rendering of legal, financial, medical or professional advice. The content within this book has been derived from various sources. Please consult a licensed professional before attempting any techniques outlined in this book.

By reading this document, the reader agrees that under no circumstances is the author responsible for any losses, direct or indirect, that are incurred as a result of the use of the information contained within this document, including, but not limited to, errors, omissions or inaccuracies.

TABLE OF CONTENTS

Table of Contents 3

Introduction 4

Chapter 1: Funny Jokes 6

Chapter 2: Crazy Jokes 18

Chapter 3: Laugh-out-Loud Jokes 30

Chapter 4: Knock-Knock Jokes 42

Chapter 5: Bonus Jokes 54

Final Words 66

INTRODUCTION

I don't know about you, but I can't think of anything better than telling a good joke.

That small pause before you tell the punchline. The look of excitement from everyone around you. The explosion of laughter at the end.

I mean, making people laugh — there is nothing better.

Which is the reason I decided to write this book in the first place.

Ever since I could remember, I simply loved telling jokes. Every spare minute I had I would be searching for new jokes I could share with my friends and family. Good jokes that would have them laughing uncontrollably as soon as I said the punchline.

But I quickly noticed that for every good joke I found, I had to read through at least ten bad ones.

I realized that the kids of the world needed a good joke book. A book of jokes where every single joke was funny. A book like this one, for example.

As a result, I spent years searching the world the world for the funniest jokes on the planet — and I think I found them all.

See in your hand you hold a book of the best jokes in the world, designed specifically for nine-year-old kids. These jokes will have you rolling around on the ground with laughter.

And even better, the jokes in this book get funnier the more you share them. Which means that you should write down your favorites so you can share them with your friends and family over and over again.

So, what are you waiting for? Start reading the funniest jokes for nine-year-old kids in the world.

Did you hear about the guy whose whole left side was cut off?

- He's all right now.

What do you call a fish wearing a suit?

- Sofishticated.

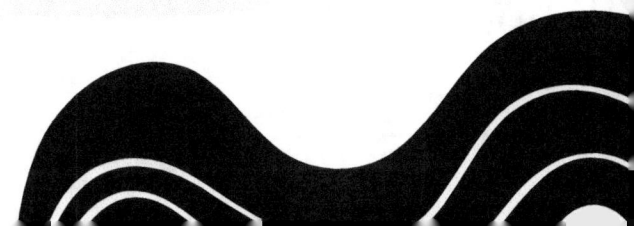

3

Why did the boy take the ruler to bed?

- **He wanted to see how long he slept.**

4

Why shouldn't you believe a person in bed?

- **Because he is lying.**

5

Why did the spider use the internet?

- **To create a website!**

6

Have you ever seen a cow with no legs? What do you think it's called?

- **Ground beef.**

What did the clam do on his birthday?

- **He shellabrated!**

What is big, has four wheels and a belly, and flies?

- **A garbage truck.**

9

Where does the electric cord go shopping?

- **At the outlet mall.**

10

Why did the coach break the vending machine?

- **Because it wasn't giving him his quarterback.**

What do you call an old goldfish?

- **Oldfish. Just remove the G.**

What is the cheetah's favorite food?

- **Fast food!**

13

What do you call a thug alligator?

- **A crook-odile.**

14

Have you heard of a rabbit that has fleas?

- **Yeah, it's Bugs bunny.**

How do you know when the moon isn't hungry?

- **When it is full.**

Where did the banana go to school?

- **Sundae school to learn how to make splits.**

(17)

I saw a man with a rubber toe. Guess what his name was!

- Roberto.

(18)

What is a shark's favorite candy?

- Jaw breakers.

19

What is a frog's favorite quote?

- **"Time is fun when you are having flies."**

20

Why did Johnny jump up and down before he drank his juice?

- **The carton said to "shake well before drinking."**

21

What did Walt Disney say when we went to the doctor?

- **Dis-knee hurts!**

22

Why did the computer go to the doctor?

- **It had a virus.**

CHAPTER 2
CRAZY JOKES

Why did the turtle struggle to get to the other side?

- **She desperately wanted to get to the Shell station.**

What did the banana do at the dance floor?

- **A banana split!**

What kind of key does a ghost use to unlock his room?

- **A spoo-key!**

What did the traffic light say to the car?

- **Don't look. I'm about to change.**

Why should you never trust stairs?

- **Because they're always up to something.**

What does the frog always order at the diner?

- **French flies!**

What do you do when 50 ghosts visit your house?

- **You hope it's Halloween!**

Why shouldn't you tell jokes about dead cellphones?

- **They just don't work.**

9

What did one elevator yell to the other?

- **I'm falling!**

10

Why do mice hate swimming?

- **They're scared of catfish.**

What do you call a can opener that doesn't work?

- A can't opener.

Why are fish healthy?

- They take vitamin sea.

13

Why did the toilet paper roll down the hill?

- **To get to the bottom.**

14

Why did the elephant quit his job at the circus?

- **He was sick of working for peanuts.**

What do you want to be when you grow up?

- **Google, because I'll have all the answers.**

On what day are twins usually born?

- **Twos-day.**

What do you call a monkey at the North Pole?

- Lost.

What do you call five giraffes?

- A high five.

Why was the baby strawberry crying?

- Because her parents were in a jam.

What did the banana say to the dog?

- Nothing; bananas can't talk.

21

What kind of lunch do moms never prepare in the morning?

- **Their own.**

22

What time is it when a ball goes through the window?

- **Time to get a new window.**

CHAPTER 3
LAUGH-OUT-LOUD JOKES

1

What did the left eye say to the right eye?

- **Between us, something smells!**

2

Why shouldn't you tell an egg a joke?

- **Because it might crack up.**

Why was school easier for cave people?

- **Because there was no history to study.**

What did the father tomato say to the baby tomato while they were out for a walk?

- **Ketchup!**

5

What's the best way to help starving monsters?

- **Give them a hand.**

6

What do you call two bananas?

- **A pair of slippers.**

What is the funniest time of the school day?

- Laughter-noon.

Why did the baker quit making donuts?

- He was just sick of the hole thing!

9

Why shouldn't you fall in love with a pastry chef?

- **They'll just DESSERT you.**

10

What tower eats a lot?

- **The I Full Tower!**

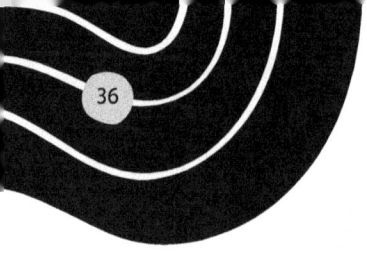

11

What do snowmen eat for breakfast?

- **Snowflakes.**

12

What did the pen say to the other pen?

- **You're ink-redible.**

13

Why didn't the teddy wear shoes to school?

- **He liked to have bear feet.**

14

Where does a ship go when it's not feeling well?

- **To see the dock-tor.**

Do zombies eat popcorn with their fingers?

- No, they eat their fingers separately!

What did you learn in school today?

- "Not enough; I have to go back tomorrow."

Why do surgeons wear masks?

- So no one will recognize them when they make a mistake.

Why did the ghost make the cheerleading squad?

- They needed team spirit.

19

Why didn't the sun go to college?

- **Because it already had a million degrees.**

20

What do baby ghosts wear on Halloween?

- **Pillowcases.**

21

Why was the car so smelly?

• It had too much gas.

22

Why did the teacher put on sunglasses?

• Because her students were so bright.

Knock, knock!

Who's there?

Warren.

Warren who?

Warren you in the same class last year?

Knock, knock!

Who's there?

Scold.

Scold who?

Scold outside! Let me in!

3

Knock, knock!

Who's there?
Tamara.

Tamara who?
Tamara is another school day. Yuk!

4

Knock, knock!

Who's there?
Will.

Will who?
I will crawl through the window if you don't open the door!

5

Knock, knock!

Who's there?
Hike.

Hike who?
I didn't know you liked Japanese poetry!

6

Knock, knock!

Who's there?
Doctor.

Doctor who?
You've seen that TV show?

Knock, knock!
Who's there?
Yah.

Yah who?
No, I prefer Google.

Knock, knock!
Who's there?
Tree.

Tree who?
Have a tree'rific day!

9

Knock, knock!
Who's there?
Cash.

Cash who?
Cash me if you can!

10

Knock, knock!
Who's there?
Vampire.

Vampire who?
Vampire (Empire) State Building!

11

Knock, knock!

Who's there?

Icing.

Icing who?

Icing so loudly everyone can hear me.

12

Knock, knock!

Who's there?

Sofa.

Sofa who?

Sofa, these have been good knock-knock jokes!

13

Knock, knock!

Who's there?

Kenya.

Kenya who?

Kenya think of anything that's more fun than geography?

14

Knock, knock!

Who's there?

Norway.

Norway who?

Norway I am telling you any more knock-knock jokes.

15

Knock, knock!

Who's there?
Allison.

Allison who?
Allison to the radio every morning! the way home?

16

Knock, knock!

Who's there?
Chile.

Chile who?
It's getting Chile out here; please let me in!

17

Knock, knock!

Who's there?

Barry.

Barry who?

Barry the treasure so no one will find it!

18

Knock, knock!

Who's there?

Carmen.

Carmen who?

Carmen get it.

19

Knock, knock!
Who's there?
Bolivia.

Bolivia who?
I Bolivia we've met!

20

Knock, knock!
Who's there?
Congo.

Congo who?
Actually, you Congo home again.

21

Knock, knock!

Who's there?
Danielle.

Danielle who?
Danielle at me; I heard you the first time.

22

Knock, knock!

Who's there?
Czech.

Czech who?
Czech your ego at the door!

1

The teacher shouted at me for something I didn't do. What was it?

- **My homework.**

2

Why did the mattress go to the doctor?

- **It had spring fever.**

Why didn't the scarecrow eat dinner?

- **He was already stuffed!**

What did one hat say to the other?

- **"You stay here, and I'll go on ahead."**

What did the balloon say to the doctor?

- I feel light-headed.

Patient: Doctor, I get heartburn every time I eat birthday cake.

- **Doctor: Next time, take off the candles.**

What kind of streets do zombies prefer?

- **Dead ends!**

What did one knife say to the other knife?

- **"You're looking sharp today!"**

9

What makes the calendar look so popular?

- It has so many dates.

10

Why did the picture go to jail?

- It was framed!

11

What did the stamp say to the envelope?

- "Stick with me, and we'll go places together."

12

What gives you the power to walk through a wall?

- A door.

13

Why couldn't the flower ride its bike to school?

- **Its petals were broken.**

14

Why can't your hand be 12 inches long?

- **Because then it would be a foot.**

Which hand is better to write with?

- **Neither! It's better to write with a pencil.**

How do they answer the phone at the paint store?

- **Yellow!**

17

Why was the baby ant confused?

- **Because all his uncles were "ants"!**

18

Why are cows so good at mathematics?

- **They use a cow-colator.**

What animal is black, white, and red?

- A zebra with a rash.

Why is there a fence around the cemetery?

- People are dying to get in.

FINAL WORDS

I really want to thank you for taking the time to read my book.

Writing this book took a very long time and a lot of work. I spent years travelling the world looking for the best jokes on the planet — and nothing makes me happier than knowing that great kids like you are reading them.

But remember, you are not done yet.

In fact, you have only just started.

Remember how I said these jokes get funnier the more times you share them? Well, it is time to share them.

Now you need to go back through the pages and pick out your favorite jokes so you can share them with your friends and family — after all, the only thing better than hearing a funny joke is telling a funny joke.

So, what are you waiting for — head back to the start and get ready to laugh all over again.

www.ingramcontent.com/pod-product-compliance
Lightning Source LLC
Chambersburg PA
CBHW072039080526
44578CB00007B/521